HOW TO START A GHOST WRITING BUSINESS

Crafting Content, Building Clients, and Achieving Success

Jeanelle K. Douglas

Copyright © 2024 by Jeanelle K. Douglas. All rights reserved. No part of this book**, How to Start a Ghostwriting Business**, may be reproduced, stored in a retrieval system, or transmitted in any form or by any means, electronic, mechanical, photocopying, recording, or otherwise, without the prior written permission of the author, Jeanelle K. Douglas.

Contents

Introduction 6
   Unravel the Art of Ghostwriting 6
   Understanding the World of Ghostwriting 8
   What Is Ghostwriting? 9
   Core Characteristics and Strength of a Ghostwriter 11
   The Role of a Ghostwriter 13
   The Evolution of Ghostwriting 15
   Ethical Considerations for Ghostwriting 18
   Opportunities and Challenges of the Ghostwriting Industry 20

Develop Your Writing Skills in the Industry 23
   Refining Your Writing Style 25
   Mastering Many Genres and Styles 28
   Research Skills for Ghostwriters 30
   Editing and Proofreading 32
   Understanding Editing versus Proofreading 32
   Collaborating with Authors: Dos and Don'ts 34

Navigating the Business of Ghostwriting 38
   Understanding Contracts and Agreements 41
   Effective Contract Management 43

Negotiating Fees and Payment Structures 45

Building a Professional Portfolio 48

Marketing Yourself as a Ghostwriter 51

Managing Client Relationships 55

Techniques for Capturing Your Client's Voice 58

Conducting Effective Interviews 61

Analyzing Existing Work for Voice and Tone 64

Using Tools and Resources to Understand Client Preferences . 67

Crafting Authentic Dialogue and Narratives 70

Feedback and Revisions: Ensuring Voice Consistency 73

Ghostwriting for Various Formats 76

Writing Books: Fiction and Non-Fiction 79

Creating Compelling Articles and Blog Posts 81

Crafting Speeches and Presentations 84

Scriptwriting for Film and Television 86

Ghostwriting in the Digital Age: Social Media, Emails, and More 89

Overcoming Challenges and Building a Successful Career 93

Dealing with Writer's Block and Creative Challenges 96

Balancing Multiple Projects and Deadlines 98

Handling Confidentiality and Discretion.................................101

Building Long-Term Relationships with Clients 103

Continuously Evolving as a Ghostwriter: Professional Development..106

Conclusion 109

Introduction

Unravel the Art of Ghostwriting

In the field of literature and communication, there is a clandestine profession that frequently works behind the scenes, creating tales, speeches, and ideas without ever taking credit.

This is the realm of ghostwriting, in which excellent wordsmiths serve as unseen conduits for other people's voices and visions. This is more than just a book; it's a thorough guide that reveals the mysteries of this enigmatic discipline, providing prospective authors with a road map to mastering the art and business of ghostwriting.

Within the pages of this book, you'll go on a voyage of discovery, delving into the varied nature of ghostwriting and the delicate balance of creativity, cooperation, and professionalism. Ghostwriting is more than just putting words on paper; it's about capturing the spirit of someone else's voice, comprehending their vision, and turning their thoughts into appealing text.

Ghostwriters must be adaptable in order to adapt to different genres, styles, and tones, whether they are writing memoirs, essays, or speeches. However, ghostwriting is not without its ethical issues. Ghostwriters must traverse a complex world of confidentiality, authorship, and integrity. Balancing client requirements with ethical considerations necessitates a thorough awareness of professional limits and a dedication to maintaining the highest standards of integrity.

This book covers all aspects of the industry, from improving your writing craft to handling the business side of ghostwriting, and will equip you to establish a successful career in this dynamic area. This book will open up a world of limitless opportunities for seasoned writers looking to broaden their horizons or new writers enticed by the attraction of ghostwriting.

So join us on a voyage of discovery as we explore the mysteries of ghostwriting and empower you to master the trade.

Understanding the World of Ghostwriting

Ghostwriting, a phrase frequently associated with mystery and intrigue, is a vocation that lives on anonymity. It is the skill of writing on behalf of another person, in which the ghostwriter's writings take on the voice of their client, perfectly fading into the background while enabling the client's thoughts and tales to shine. Ghostwriting is really about collaboration and symbiosis.

Ghostwriters collaborate closely with their customers to grasp their distinct voice, perspective, and goals, transforming into literary chameleons capable of adapting their writing style to that of their clients. Ghostwriters must be able to accurately and precisely channel their clients' voices while writing memoirs, essays, speeches, or books.

A ghostwriter's job entails more than just writing; it also demands a thorough command of storytelling, narrative structure, and linguistic intricacies. Ghostwriters must be talented researchers who can delve into a variety of themes and turn difficult material into intriguing narratives. They must also be skilled editors, ensuring that their work is clear, coherent, and consistent with the client's voice. Ghostwriting is a profession with a long history, stretching back centuries to when scribes wrote letters, speeches, and manuscripts for their clients.

Ghostwriting now covers a wide range of mediums and genres, including traditional books and essays as well as digital material and social media postings.

However, ghostwriting is not without ethical implications. The invisibility of the ghostwriter creates issues of authorship, ownership, and transparency. Ethical ghostwriting necessitates a fine balance between meeting the client's demands and maintaining the integrity of the written word.

What Is Ghostwriting?

Ghostwriting is a complex and multidimensional business that centers on the art of writing on behalf of another person while remaining anonymous or uncredited. Ghostwriters are essentially literary partners who utilize their writing abilities to give voice to other people's ideas, stories, and viewpoints.

This invisible relationship enables customers to use the knowledge of a competent writer to bring their ideas to life without having to devote the time or effort to writing themselves. Ghostwriting is fundamentally about capturing the essence of the client's voice and vision and then converting those thoughts and ideas into appealing text. This necessitates a thorough awareness of the client's goals, audience, and style, as well as the ability to smoothly alter one's writing to match the client's voice.

Ghostwriters must be versatile and skilled enough to create compelling and authentic material that connects with the client's target audience, whether they are writing a memoir, an essay, a speech, or a book. Ghostwriting covers a wide range of genres and channels, including traditional print publications, internet articles, and social media posts. Ghostwriters may work with customers from a variety of sectors and backgrounds, including corporate executives, celebrities, academics, and thought leaders, to mention a few.

Each assignment brings unique obstacles and possibilities, necessitating ghostwriters' adaptability, resourcefulness, and creativity. While ghostwriting has several advantages for customers, including time savings, professional polish, and access to experienced writing talent, it also raises ethical concerns about authorship and transparency. Ghostwriters must manage these ethical quandaries with honesty and professionalism, maintaining the highest levels of secrecy and respecting the client's desires about credit.

This book, decipher the complexities of ghostwriting, from knowing the principles to mastering the skills and strategies required for success. It provide prospective ghostwriters with practical ideas, real-world examples, and ethical concerns to help them navigate this dynamic and profitable industry with confidence and integrity.

This is the essential guide for both seasoned writers seeking to expand their skill set and beginners captivated by the allure of ghostwriting. It will help you master the art and business of writing in the shadows, where words transform into whispers and stories come alive through the hands of invisible scribes.

Core Characteristics and Strength of a Ghostwriter

Ghostwriting, at its core, is a type of narrative in which the ghostwriter's function goes beyond that of a mere scribe. It entails putting oneself in the shoes of the customer, understanding their point of view, and weaving their story in such a manner that it accurately expresses their essence. This requires not just outstanding writing abilities but also sensitivity, intuition, and a deep grasp of human emotions and experiences.

One of the distinguishing characteristics of ghostwriting is its obscurity. Unlike conventional authors, who are recognized for their work, ghostwriters stay nameless or are credited with the client's name. This anonymity enables customers to take custody of their work while exploiting the ghostwriter's experience and creativity. It also needs ghostwriters to put their egos aside and emphasize the client's goals over their own desire for notoriety.

Ghostwriting is a collaborative activity that frequently requires close contact and feedback between the ghostwriter and the client. This cooperation may take many forms, ranging from early brainstorming meetings to regular check-ins and modifications throughout the writing process. Effective communication is essential for ensuring that the end result reflects the client's vision and satisfies their expectations.

Ghostwriters must be good at research in addition to writing and cooperation. Depending on the subject, this might include researching historical archives, conducting interviews, or analyzing data to verify accuracy and authenticity. Research not only improves the quality of the writing, but it also allows ghostwriters to obtain a better grasp of the subject matter and the client's viewpoint.

Ghostwriting involves major ethical problems, notably in terms of secrecy and attribution. Ghostwriters must be entrusted with sensitive material and abide by rigorous confidentiality agreements to preserve their customers' privacy. In addition, ghostwriters must make clear and ethical judgments on attribution, considering the client's preferences and the nature of the project.

The Role of a Ghostwriter

Ghostwriting is a complicated career that necessitates a diversified skill set and a distinct approach to writing. A ghostwriter's primary function is to serve as a conduit for another person's voice, ideas, and tales. This is far more than simply putting pen to paper; it necessitates a thorough grasp of the client's objectives, audience, and style, as well as the ability to tailor one's writing to perfectly match the client's voice. A ghostwriter's primary responsibility is to capture the essence of their client's voice and vision.

This means immersing oneself in the client's point of view, understanding their motives and goals, and translating their thoughts and ideas into compelling and real language. Whether writing a biography, an essay, a speech, or a book, the ghostwriter must channel the client's voice with accuracy and authenticity to ensure that the finished product speaks to the desired audience.

Ghostwriters are responsible for both capturing the client's voice and safeguarding the anonymity of their clients' information. Clients frequently engage ghostwriters with sensitive personal or professional information, and it is critical that ghostwriters follow tight confidentiality agreements to safeguard their clients' privacy and confidence. Collaboration is another important component of a ghostwriter's function. Ghostwriters collaborate with their customers throughout the writing process, from the first brainstorming meetings to regular check-ins and edits.

Effective communication and teamwork are critical for ensuring that the final result reflects the client's vision and fulfills their expectations. Furthermore, ghostwriters must have great research abilities in order to obtain essential material and guarantee that their writing is accurate and authentic. Depending on the project, this might include conducting interviews, researching historical archives, or analyzing statistics to support the client's story.

Whether you're interested in the potential of giving your voice to others' stories or looking to develop your writing talents and extend your professional horizons, this book is your definitive guide to mastering the job of the ghostwriter and becoming a master of the invisible pen. Join us on this trip as we unearth the secrets of ghostwriting and enable you to flourish in this dynamic and lucrative industry.

The Evolution of Ghostwriting

The art of ghostwriting has evolved significantly over time, responding to shifts in technology, culture, and the publishing industry. The evolution of ghostwriting from a service performed by scribes and secretaries to the sophisticated profession it is today reflects larger advances in communication, narrative, and the nature of authorship.

Ghostwriting dates back to ancient times, when scribes and scholars wrote letters, speeches, and manuscripts for rulers, politicians, and other prominent figures. These ghostwriters played an important part in influencing their clients' narratives and messages, frequently staying unknown or unacknowledged for their work.

Ghostwriting became more popular in the modern era as mass media and the publishing industry developed. As demand for content increased, particularly for celebrity memoirs and political speeches, ghostwriters began to play a larger role in shaping public discourse. Despite making major contributions, ghostwriters often remained concealed behind the scenes, their identities absent from the bylines of the works they assisted in producing.

The internet and digital publication have further altered the terrain of ghostwriting, creating new opportunities and problems for authors. With the rise of blogs, online publications, and social media platforms, ghostwriters found themselves in great demand, creating material for corporations, influencers, and people trying to develop a digital footprint.

Ghostwriting now covers a wide range of genres and channels, including traditional books and essays as well as digital material and social media postings. Ghostwriters work with customers from a variety of backgrounds, including corporate executives, celebrities, academics, and thought leaders, to create captivating tales that connect with their audiences. The growth of ghostwriting has also prompted fundamental ethical questions about authorship, ownership, and transparency.

As ghostwriters continue to influence public discourse, questions about attribution and accountability have become more pressing. Ethical ghostwriting necessitates a fine balance between meeting the client's demands and maintaining the integrity of the written word. If you're interested in the history of ghostwriting or want to grasp its current significance, this book provides useful insights and practical advice for navigating this dynamic and developing business.

Changes in reader tastes, technical improvements, and the advent of self-publishing platforms have influenced the growth of ghostwriting in the publishing business. With the rise of self-publishing possibilities, authors have increasingly turned to ghostwriters to help them bring their ideas to life, avoiding traditional publishing gatekeepers and preserving more control over their work.

The globalization of communication has created new chances for ghostwriters to work with customers from all over the world. Technology has made it simpler than ever for writers to communicate with customers remotely, providing greater flexibility and diversity in the types of work handled. As the environment of ghostwriting evolves, so do the talents and attributes necessary to flourish in the industry. Ghostwriters must have good research skills, versatility, and a thorough awareness of numerous sectors and subject subjects.

Ethical Considerations for Ghostwriting

Ghostwriting, while a beneficial service that allows people to express their experiences and ideas, poses various ethical issues that ghostwriters must negotiate with honesty and skill.

These factors include questions of authorship, secrecy, transparency, and honesty, among others.

One of the most important ethical issues in ghostwriting is authorship. Ghostwriters frequently stay nameless or are credited with the client's name, raising concerns about transparency and ownership of the work.

While ghostwriters play an important part in molding the material, clients eventually claim credit for the work, which can lead to misconceptions or misrepresentations of authorship.

Confidentiality is another important ethical concern in ghostwriting. Customers often supply ghostwriters with sensitive material, including personal anecdotes, professional experiences, and confidential information.

Ghostwriters must follow tight confidentiality agreements to safeguard their clients' privacy and confidence. Transparency is critical for understanding the ethical challenges of ghostwriting. It is important to inform clients about the ghostwriter's function and level of engagement in the project. This includes addressing concerns like attribution, cooperation, and confidentiality boundaries early on to promote clarity and mutual understanding.

Honesty is essential for establishing trust and integrity in ghostwriting. When dealing with customers, ghostwriters must be open and honest about their skills, expertise, and qualifications. They should correctly describe their talents and knowledge, avoid distortion or embellishment, and be open about the extent and limitations of their services.

Another ethical aspect of ghostwriting is to convey the client's voice and perspective. Ghostwriters must aim to accurately capture the spirit of the client's speech without imposing their own prejudices or agendas. This necessitates active listening, empathy, and a dedication to understanding the client's viewpoint and goals.

Opportunities and Challenges of the Ghostwriting Industry

The ghostwriting industry provides several options for authors looking to broaden their horizons and make a significant impact with their work. However, these prospects bring with them a unique set of hurdles that prospective ghostwriters must overcome with tenacity, ingenuity, and dedication.

Opportunities

1. Diverse Projects: Ghostwriters can work on a wide range of projects across genres, styles, and mediums. From memoirs and biographies to essays, speeches, and digital material, authors have plenty of possibilities to demonstrate their diversity and inventiveness.

2. Collaboration with Diverse Clients: Ghostwriters work with customers from a variety of backgrounds and professions, including corporate executives, celebrities, professors, and thought leaders. This allows authors to obtain insights into numerous professions, broaden their professional networks, and learn from specialists in diverse domains.

3. Flexibility and Autonomy: Ghostwriting allows writers to work on their own time and from almost anywhere on the globe. This freedom enables authors to pursue additional hobbies, manage several projects, and customize their jobs to their lifestyle and tastes.

4. Professional Development: Working as a ghostwriter offers authors several options for professional development and advancement. Writers can improve their writing talents, acquire new techniques, and receive experience in a variety of facets of the publishing industry, including research, editing, marketing, and promotion.

Challenges

1. Confidentiality Issues: Ghostwriters frequently deal with sensitive information and must follow rigorous confidentiality agreements to preserve their customers' privacy. Balancing the requirement for anonymity with openness and responsibility may be difficult, so ghostwriters must develop clear communication and trust with their clients.

2. Ethical Considerations: Ghostwriting raises ethical questions about authorship, credit, and transparency. Ghostwriters must manage these ethical quandaries with integrity and professionalism, maintaining the highest levels of honesty, openness, and respect for their customers' demands.

3. Client Management: Managing client relationships may be difficult, especially when dealing with various personalities, interests, and expectations. Ghostwriters must communicate effectively, establish clear limits, and manage expectations to maintain a healthy and fruitful working relationship with their customers.

4. Navigating the Business Side: Ghostwriters must understand the business aspect of ghostwriting, which includes negotiating pricing and contracts, managing funds, and effectively marketing their services. To thrive in this competitive field, you must have a combination of business acumen, negotiation skills, and marketing expertise.

Develop Your Writing Skills in the Industry

In the fast-paced and competitive world of ghostwriting, improving and sharpening your writing abilities is critical to success. As a ghostwriter, your ability to create intriguing storylines, capture multiple voices, and adapt to different genres and styles will distinguish you and propel your work to new heights.

Understanding your craft

Developing your writing talents starts with a thorough comprehension of the discipline of writing itself. This involves learning the principles of grammar, syntax, and punctuation, as well as developing your ability to write clear and compelling phrases and paragraphs. Familiarizing yourself with various writing styles, genres, and storytelling strategies can extend your creative toolbox and increase your versatility as a writer.

Ghostwriters frequently rely on their versatility to write in a variety of genres, styles, and mediums. Versatility is essential while writing a memoir, an essay, or a speech. Developing the capacity to tailor your writing style to your clients' tone, voice, and objectives will allow you to approach any job with confidence and professionalism.

Research skills:

Effective research is an essential component of the ghostwriting process, allowing you to collect information, check facts, and improve the depth and authenticity of your work. Developing great research abilities includes understanding where and how to obtain credible sources, performing extensive investigations, and combining complicated material into cohesive narratives. Cultivating a desire for learning and a thorough attention to detail will help you succeed in your research pursuits.

Editing and Proofreading: The ability to edit and proofread your work is critical for maintaining clarity, coherence, and correctness in your writing. Developing great editing and proofreading abilities entails improving your awareness of grammar and style rules, as well as your attention to detail and critical eye for mistakes.

Self-editing approaches and obtaining input from peers or mentors can help you fine-tune your editing abilities and improve the quality of your work.

Cooperation and communication: Ghostwriters must be able to collaborate and communicate effectively since they frequently work closely with clients to bring their thoughts to reality.

Active listening, clear concept articulation, and the capacity to offer and receive constructive feedback are all necessary for developing excellent communication skills. Cultivating a collaborative mentality and maintaining open lines of contact with your clients can help guarantee that your writing achieves their expectations and objectives.

Refining Your Writing Style

In the dynamic and complex world of ghostwriting, perfecting your writing style is critical for creating your own voice and leaving an indelible impact on your readers. Your writing style includes not just the words you use and sentence structure but also the tone, voice, and general approach to narrative.

Developing a distinct and captivating writing style can help you stand out as a ghostwriter and increase the impact of your work. Understanding your audience: Understanding your audience is an important first step in improving your writing style. Whether you're writing for a corporate executive, a celebrity, or an academic, you must customize your writing style to match your audience's tastes, expectations, and degree of experience.

Understanding your audience's demographics, interests, and motives will help you make style decisions and guarantee that your writing resonates with them on a deeper level.

Find Your Voice: Developing your writing style also entails discovering your own distinct voice as a writer. Your voice reflects your personality, perspective, and ideals, influencing the tone and authenticity of your work. Experimenting with numerous writing techniques, genres, and mediums, as well as reflecting on your own experiences and views, will help you discover and polish your voice as a writer.

Creating Compelling Prose: Honing your writing style entails mastering the skill of creating interesting text that captivates and interests your readers. This entails paying attention to characteristics like timing, rhythm, and imagery, as well as selecting words that elicit emotion and generate vivid mental images. Developing a strong sense of storytelling and narrative structure will allow you to create engaging and memorable reading experiences for your readers.

Adjusting to various genres and styles: Ghostwriters often write in a variety of genres, styles, and mediums. Developing the capacity to tailor your writing style to the individual needs of each client is critical for success in the ghostwriting profession. Whether you're writing a gripping thriller, an emotional memoir, or a thought-provoking piece, being able to flip between genres and tones will show your variety and expertise as a writer.

Refine Your Editing Skills: Another key component of developing your writing style is improving your editing abilities. Editing is an important component of the writing process since it entails rewriting, clarifying, and polishing your work to guarantee clarity, coherence, and effectiveness. Developing great editing abilities includes checking your work for grammar, punctuation, and syntax, as well as style, tone, and overall effect. Practicing self-editing strategies and obtaining feedback from peers or mentors will help you improve your editing abilities and the quality of your work. Join us as we explore the complexities of writing in the dark and prepare you to become a master of the invisible pen.

Mastering Many Genres and Styles

Mastering many genres and styles as a ghostwriter, you must learn many genres and styles in order to meet your customers' unique demands and tastes. Each project has its own set of obstacles and requirements, including tone and voice, narrative structure, and pacing. Developing the ability to write well in a variety of genres and styles can not only demonstrate your diversity as a writer but also increase your worth and attractiveness as a ghostwriter.

Understanding Genre Conventions: Mastering multiple genres requires a thorough awareness of genre rules and expectations. Whether you're creating fiction, nonfiction, or creative material, each genre has its own set of rules, clichés, and narrative strategies. Familiarizing yourself with these standards can help you write realistic and compelling stories that people will like.

Adapting Your Writing Style: Adapting your writing style to meet the particular needs of each genre is critical to your success as a ghostwriter. Whether you're writing a scary thriller, a romantic romance, or a thought-provoking self-help book, your ability to flip between diverse styles and tones will show your versatility and skill as a writer. This entails paying attention to features like pacing, dialogue, and character development, as well as selecting words and phrases that convey the right tone and atmosphere for the genre.

Researching genre trends: Staying up-to-date on current trends and advancements in many genres is critical for successful mastery. This entails reading extensively within each genre, evaluating best-selling books and prominent writers, and staying current on audience preferences and market trends. Understanding the changing landscape of each genre will allow you to anticipate and adapt to shifting reader expectations, keeping your writing fresh and entertaining.

Experimenting with different styles: Mastering diverse genres and styles entails experimenting with various writing strategies and approaches. Whether you're writing in a formal, academic style or in a casual, conversational tone, you must be able to tailor your writing to the demands of your customers and their intended audience. To develop memorable and effective writing, you may want to experiment with multiple narrative viewpoints, play with language and imagery, and investigate unique storytelling strategies.

Seeking feedback and iteration: Seeking input from peers, mentors, and clients is an essential component of mastering diverse genres and styles. Soliciting comments on your writing helps you acquire useful insights into areas for growth and enhance your abilities as needed. Being open to feedback and eager to iterate on your writing will allow you to constantly develop and expand as a writer, ultimately increasing the quality and effectiveness of your work across genres and styles.

Research Skills for Ghostwriters

Ghostwriters must have strong research abilities to obtain information, verify facts, and ensure the correctness and authenticity of their work. Ghostwriters are frequently assigned to write on a broad range of topics and sectors, and their ability to undertake extensive and comprehensive research has a direct impact on the quality and authenticity of their work. Conducting Comprehensive Research Ghostwriters must be able to perform extensive studies on a number of themes. This entails consulting a variety of sources, such as books, academic publications, credible websites, and conversations with subject-matter experts. Ghostwriters may improve the credibility of their work by extensively studying their themes and generating well-informed, factually correct content.

Verifying the Facts and Information: In addition to acquiring research, ghostwriters must be capable of validating facts and information to assure its accuracy. This may entail cross-referencing several sources, reviewing original sources if available, and double-checking information with credible sources. Ghostwriters should prevent flaws and errors that could jeopardize the legitimacy of their work by double-checking their information.

Analyze and synthesize information: Ghostwriters must also be able to effectively evaluate and synthesize enormous volumes of information. This entails discovering essential insights, trends, and patterns in the research data and integrating them into coherent and captivating narratives. Ghostwriters may express difficult ideas and concepts in a straightforward and engaging manner by evaluating and synthesizing material, increasing their writing's readability and effect.

Aligning Research to Client Needs: Ghostwriters must be able to tailor their research to the individual demands and interests of their customers. This may entail adapting the breadth and extent of their research to match the client's goals, readership, and writing style. Ghostwriters may guarantee that their work matches the particular criteria of each assignment while also effectively addressing the client's aims by tailoring their research technique.

Keeping up with trends and developments: Finally, ghostwriters must keep up with trends and advances in their sector or specialization. This might include tracking industry journals, attending conferences and seminars, and following important thought leaders and influencers. Ghostwriters may keep their work relevant and up-to-date by remaining on top of current trends and developments, increasing its value and reader appeal.

Editing and Proofreading

Editing and proofreading are essential steps in the ghostwriting process, ensuring that the final written product is polished, error-free, and ready for publication. As a ghostwriter, understanding editing and proofreading processes is critical for producing high-quality work that fulfills your customers' expectations and resonates with their target audience.

Understanding Editing versus Proofreading

It is critical for ghostwriters to recognize the difference between editing and proofreading. Editing is the process of examining and editing information for clarity, coherence, structure, tone, and overall effectiveness.

This might include rearranging paragraphs, rewriting phrases, tightening wording, and correcting any inconsistencies or gaps in the story. Proofreading, on the other hand, aims to rectify problems in grammar, punctuation, spelling, and formatting. Proofreading guarantees that the final written product is accurate and correct, whereas editing addresses larger concerns of content and style.

Developing a Systematic Approach: Effective editing and proofreading need a methodical approach to ensure completeness and correctness. Ghostwriters should create a disciplined process that involves several rounds of editing and proofreading. This may include starting with substantive adjustments to address broader concerns of content and style, then moving on to line edits to polish language and enhance readability, and finally proofreading to spot any residual errors.

Taking breaks between revisions: To retain neutrality and efficacy during the editing and proofreading process, ghostwriters should take breaks between revisions. Stepping away from the writing offers a new perspective and identifies opportunities for improvement that may have gone unnoticed during prior rounds of editing. Taking pauses also helps to reduce weariness, allowing ghostwriters to approach the editing and proofreading process with renewed focus and attention to detail.

Using Editing Tools and Resources: In addition to manual editing and proofreading, ghostwriters can use a range of tools and resources to improve their editing process. This might include grammar and spell-checking software, style guides, writing instructions, and online editing tools. These tools can help speed up the editing and proofreading process, spot frequent problems, and make useful suggestions for enhancing writing style and clarity.

Looking for feedback from peers and mentors: Another effective editing strategy for ghostwriters is to solicit input from peers and mentors. Collaboration with other authors and industry professionals enables ghostwriters to obtain new views, detect blind spots, and receive critical feedback on their work. Peer feedback may help identify areas for development while also providing vital ideas on how to improve the overall quality and effectiveness of written work.

Reading Aloud with Multiple Passes: Reading aloud is an effective editing approach that enables ghostwriters to notice odd language, imprecise phrases, and grammatical faults that might otherwise go undetected while reading silently. Furthermore, making many passes through the editing and proofreading process improves thoroughness and correctness. Each pass can concentrate on different elements of editing and proofreading, such as content, style, grammar, punctuation, and formatting, allowing ghostwriters to tackle each one methodically and successfully.

Collaborating with Authors: Dos and Don'ts

Working with writers as a ghostwriter is a sensitive and difficult process that involves efficient communication, mutual respect, and a clear knowledge of expectations. In order to promote a happy and productive working environment, it is important to follow certain dos and don'ts when navigating this collaborative partnership.

Do's:

1. Establish Clear Communication: Effective communication is essential for a successful partnership with writers. Create open and clear communication channels from the start, outlining expectations, timetables, project scope, and any special preferences or rules. Regularly inform the author of the project's progress and respond to their feedback and ideas.

2. Listen To And Understand Their Vision: Take the time to hear the author's vision for the project and comprehend their aims, ambitions, and expectations. Ask clarifying questions to obtain a better grasp of their vision, and actively incorporate their criticism and ideas into your own work. Strive to capture their voice and perspective honestly, so that the end result reflects their vision.

3. Respect Their Expertise and Input: Recognize and value the author's skills and contributions throughout the collaborative process. Acknowledge their expertise in the subject area and sector, and use their suggestions to improve the quality and authenticity of your work. Collaborate with the author like a partner, recognizing their contributions and treating them equally in the creative process.

4. Be Flexible and Adaptable: Flexibility is necessary when working with writers since projects might evolve or shift direction over time. Be open to criticism and prepared to change your approach to match the author's requirements and preferences. Be proactive in responding to any complaints or difficulties that occur, and be adaptable in accommodating modifications or alterations as needed.

5. Maintain Professionalism and Confidentiality: Maintain professionalism and secrecy throughout the collaborative process. Respect the author's privacy and confidentiality, especially if working on delicate or personal projects. Adhere to any confidentiality or non-disclosure agreements (NDAs) that may be in place, and always respect the author's confidence and secrecy.

Don'ts:

1. Imposing Your Own Agenda: Avoid imposing your own goal or artistic vision on the project without first considering the author's suggestions and preferences. Respect the author's vision and aims, and endeavor to make your work consistent with their goals and expectations. Collaboration should be founded on mutual respect and understanding, not a unilateral imposition of your own views.

2. Disregarding Feedback: Ignoring or ignoring the author's input is a certain way to derail the collaborative partnership. Be open to constructive criticism and comments, and be prepared to revise or change depending on the author's suggestions. Express gratitude for their criticism and a readiness to incorporate their recommendations into your work.

3. Missing Deadlines and Deliverables: Failure to achieve deadlines or deliverables can undermine trust and confidence in a collaborative partnership. Respect the agreed-upon schedules and deliverables, and communicate proactively if there are any delays or issues. Strive to do high-quality work on time and within the stated constraints, exhibiting your dependability and expertise as a ghostwriter.

4. Overstepping Boundaries: Avoid overstepping limits or exceeding the project's scope without the author's permission. Respect any constraints or limitations established by the author, whether they relate to the project's substance, style, or direction. Clarify expectations and scope of work upfront to guarantee a clear understanding of roles and duties, and avoid making unilateral choices that may have an influence on the project without first engaging the author.

5. Compromising. Confidentiality: Maintaining secrecy is critical when dealing with writers, particularly on delicate or personal projects. Do not share or disclose any sensitive or proprietary information without the author's explicit consent. Respect any confidentiality agreements or NDAs, and emphasize the author's privacy and secrecy throughout the collaborative process.

Navigating the Business of Ghostwriting

To compete in the competitive ghostwriting market, you must have a combination of writing talents, business knowledge, and professionalism. As a ghostwriter, you are responsible not only for producing high-quality writing but also for overseeing different elements of your business, such as client relationships, pricing, contracts, and marketing. Understanding the industry environment, building a good professional reputation, and efficiently managing your business operations are all necessary for success in the ghostwriting business.

Understanding the Industry Landscape: To properly manage the ghostwriting business, you must first comprehend the industry environment. This involves understanding current market trends, the need for ghostwriter services, and industry competitiveness. Stay current on industry advancements, developing trends, and new possibilities that may affect your business. Researching potential clients, understanding their needs, and recognizing specialized markets may all help you position yourself effectively in the sector.

Building a Professional Reputation: Building a great professional reputation is critical to succeeding in the ghostwriting industry. Your reputation as a trustworthy, knowledgeable, and professional ghostwriter will attract clients and distinguish you from the competition. To establish trust and reputation in the industry, focus on producing high-quality work, meeting deadlines, and surpassing customer expectations. Encourage delighted customers to offer comments or references that will demonstrate your knowledge and dependability to prospective prospects.

Setting rates and negotiating contracts: Setting your prices and negotiating contracts are critical components of managing the ghostwriting industry. Set fees that represent the value of your job, taking into account your degree of expertise, project complexity, and the client's budget. Negotiate contracts that explicitly define the project scope, deliverables, timetables, payment arrangements, and any other applicable terms and conditions. Prepare to negotiate with clients to reach a mutually advantageous deal that fits both parties' needs.

Manage Client Relationships: Effective client management is important for success in the ghostwriting industry. Communicate openly and professionally with customers, defining expectations and offering regular project updates. Be receptive to client input and willing to make tweaks or adjustments as needed to achieve client satisfaction. Building excellent customer connections may lead to repeat business and referrals, which will help your ghostwriting business expand and succeed.

Marketing and Promoting Your Services: Promoting your ghostwriting services is critical for recruiting clients and expanding your business. Create a complete marketing plan that combines both online and offline strategies to reach your intended demographic. This may include developing a professional website or portfolio to showcase your work, connecting with potential clients via social media platforms, attending industry events or networking opportunities, and using content marketing tactics like blogging or guest posting to demonstrate your expertise and attract clients.

Manage Business Operations: Navigating the ghostwriting industry also requires excellent management of different parts of your company's operations. This involves managing administrative chores including billing, bookkeeping, and project management, as well as keeping orderly records of client correspondence, contracts, and project information. Use tools and resources like project management software, accounting software, and online invoicing platforms to simplify your business operations and maintain professionalism and efficiency in your daily activities.

Understanding Contracts and Agreements

Understanding contracts and agreements is critical for ghostwriters to safeguard their rights, clarify expectations, and maintain a mutually productive relationship with customers. Contracts are legally binding agreements that define the terms and circumstances of a ghostwriting job, including project scope, deliverables, timeframes, payment terms, and confidentiality agreements.

To successfully manage the commercial aspect of ghostwriting, ghostwriters must have a deep grasp of contracts and agreements.

Key Components of Contracts and Agreements:

1. Project Scope: Contracts should explicitly outline the scope of the ghostwriting assignment, including the sort of writing services to be delivered, the precise deliverables (e.g., manuscripts, articles, blog posts), and any optional services (e.g., research, revisions).

2. Deliverables: Contracts should specify the particular deliverables required from the ghostwriter, including the format, duration, and date for each one. This ensures that all parties have a thorough grasp of the project's requirements and timetables.

3. Timelines: Contracts should provide dates or deadlines for finishing the project, including milestones for submitting drafts, changes, and final deliverables. Establishing defined timeframes helps to manage expectations and ensure that the project runs smoothly and on time.

4. Payment conditions: Contracts should contain the payment conditions for the ghostwriting project, including the total project price, payment schedule (e.g., initial deposit, installment payments), and any extra fees or expenditures (e.g., research costs, travel expenses) that may arise. Clearly establishing payment conditions helps to minimize misunderstandings and assures fast payment for services provided.

5. Confidentiality Agreements: Contracts may contain confidentiality agreements or non-disclosure agreements (NDAs) to safeguard the client's intellectual information or sensitive materials. Ghostwriters frequently have access to personal material; thus, confidentiality agreements help protect client privacy and prevent the unlawful publication of sensitive information.

6. Copyright and Ownership: Contracts should include provisions for the copyright and ownership of literary material created by the ghostwriter. Depending on the terms of the contract, the client may keep complete ownership and copyright of the work, while the ghostwriter may retain certain rights or earn acknowledgment for their work. It's crucial to specify ownership rights upfront to avoid conflicts over intellectual property rights later on.

7. Termination provision: Contracts should include a termination provision that describes the conditions under which either party can cancel the agreement and the method for doing so. This gives a means for resolving conflicts or dissolving the partnership peacefully if required.

8. Legal Considerations: Prepare contracts in line with the laws and regulations that govern contracts in the relevant country. It's important to contact a legal expert or contract lawyer to verify that contracts are legally enforceable and effectively safeguard the interests of both parties.

Effective Contract Management

1. Review contracts carefully: Before signing any contract or agreement, thoroughly consider the terms and conditions to ensure that you completely understand your rights and duties. Pay particular attention to crucial elements such as project scope, deliverables, payment conditions, and confidentiality agreements.

2. Seek legal advice: If you have any issues or questions regarding a contract or agreement, get legal guidance from a knowledgeable attorney or contract lawyer. A legal practitioner may evaluate the contract, give information on any risks or obligations, and assist in negotiating favorable terms if required.

3. Maintain copies of contracts: Keep copies of any contracts and agreements relating to your ghostwriting work for your records. This includes signed contracts, modifications, and any communication relating to contract talks or updates.

4. Communicate Openly: Maintain open and transparent communication with clients throughout the contract negotiation process. Clearly clarify your expectations, answer any issues or questions, and confirm that all parties are in agreement on the terms of the contract before advancing.

5. Adhere to Contract Terms: After signing a contract, it is important to adhere to the terms and conditions mentioned in the agreement. This involves fulfilling project deadlines, producing high-quality work, and complying with confidentiality agreements and other contractual commitments.

Negotiating Fees and Payment Structures

Negotiating pricing and payment systems is a vital component of the ghostwriting industry since it directly affects the financial aspects of the project and the overall profitability of the ghostwriter. Successfully negotiating prices and payment systems needs a mix of recognizing your worth as a writer, estimating the value of the job, and effectively engaging with customers to create a mutually beneficial agreement.

Understanding Your Worth: Before starting to have discussions with a client, it's crucial to have a clear sense of your worth as a ghostwriter. This involves examining aspects such as your degree of experience and knowledge, the complexity of the project, and the value you bring to the table. Take into account your skill level, reputation, and track record of producing high-quality work when deciding your cost structure.

Assessing the Value of the Project: When discussing costs and payment arrangements, it's vital to analyze the worth of the project to decide a suitable charge. Consider aspects such as the extent and complexity of the project, the time and effort necessary to execute it, and the possible influence of your work on the client's goals and objectives. Take into consideration any additional services or value-added items you may supply, such as research, edits, or consulting services.

Researching Industry Standards: Researching industry norms and market prices for ghostwriting services can give significant insights regarding pricing and fee structures. Investigate what other ghostwriters with similar experience and abilities are charging for comparable assignments. This can help you create competitive pricing that represents the market value of your services while also ensuring that you are reimbursed appropriately for your labor.

Tailoring Payment Structures: When discussing payment arrangements, consider adjusting the conditions to meet both your demands and the client's budget and preferences. Common payment formats for ghostwriting assignments include upfront deposits, milestone payments depending on project milestones or deliverables, and installment payments spread out throughout the life of the job. Be flexible and open to exploring other payment choices to find a solution that works for both sides.

Communicating Value: Effectively articulating the value of your services is crucial to negotiating rates and payment systems successfully. Clearly define the advantages and outcomes that the customer will obtain from your ghostwriting services, stressing the value that your knowledge and abilities provide to the project. Highlight your track record of producing high-quality work, meeting deadlines, and surpassing customer expectations to illustrate the worth of your services.

Negotiating Terms and Conditions: During talks, be prepared to discuss and negotiate the terms and conditions of the project, including costs, payment methods, project scope, deliverables, timetables, and any extra services or requirements. Be forceful in arguing for your interests and requirements while also being prepared to compromise and find common ground with the customer. Keep the lines of communication open and maintain a collaborative attitude toward negotiations to guarantee a beneficial conclusion for all sides.

Documenting Agreements: Once an agreement has been made, write down the terms and conditions in a formal contract or agreement. Clearly explain the agreed-upon prices, payment methods, project scope, deliverables, timeframes, and any other applicable terms and conditions. Having a written contract helps eliminate misunderstandings and disagreements down the line and gives a clear reference point for both parties.

Building a Professional Portfolio

Ghostwriters must create a professional portfolio to demonstrate their skills, experience, and expertise to potential clients and establish industry credibility. A well-curated portfolio not only highlights your writing skills, but it also demonstrates your versatility, professionalism, and ability to deliver high-quality work in a variety of genres and industries.

Here's a thorough overview of how to create a professional portfolio as a ghostwriter:

1. **Selecting Your Best Work:** Begin by selecting the best writing samples to include in your portfolio. Choose pieces that demonstrate your writing style, voice, and versatility across genres and formats. Choose samples that demonstrate your ability to adapt your writing to the needs of different clients and audiences.

2. **Showcase Variety:** Showcase your versatility by including a variety of writing samples in your portfolio. This could include articles, blog posts, essays, website content, marketing materials, social media posts, speeches, whitepapers, case studies, and other pertinent materials. Showcasing a variety of writing styles and formats helps prospective clients understand the scope of your ghostwriting abilities.

3. **Highlighting client success stories:** If possible, include testimonials or success stories from previous clients to boost the credibility of your portfolio. Client testimonials provide social proof of your abilities and reassure potential clients about your dependability, professionalism, and effectiveness as a ghostwriter. Include brief case studies or client testimonials that demonstrate how you contributed to successful projects and satisfied clients.

4. **Tailoring Your Portfolio for Your Target Audience:** Consider your target audience and design your portfolio accordingly. If you specialize in a particular niche or industry, include writing samples that are appropriate for that audience. Highlight your expertise in business, finance, health, technology, education, or any other area in which you specialize. Tailoring your portfolio to your target audience allows you to leave a stronger impression and attract clients in your field of expertise.

5. **Organizing Your Portfolio:** Organize your portfolio in a professional, visually appealing manner. Make a separate section for each type of writing sample, and include a brief description or context for each one. Consider combining text, images, and multimedia elements to improve the presentation of your portfolio. Use clear headings,

subheadings, and formatting to make your portfolio easy to navigate and visually appealing.

6. **Creating an Online Portfolio:** Consider creating an online portfolio to share your work with a larger audience. A professional website or online portfolio allows you to showcase your writing samples, client testimonials, and contact information in one convenient location. Choose a clean and user-friendly design for your website and optimize it for search engines to increase visibility and attract new customers.

7. **Updating Your Portfolio Frequently:** Keep your portfolio up to date by regularly adding new writing samples and removing old or irrelevant content. As you gain experience and complete new projects, update your portfolio to reflect your most recent work and accomplishments. Regularly refreshing your portfolio demonstrates your continued development and dedication to excellence as a ghostwriter.

8. **Promote Your Portfolio:** Once you've built your professional portfolio, actively promote it to potential clients. Share links to your portfolio on social media, professional networking websites, and online writing communities. Consider contacting potential clients directly and sharing your portfolio with them to demonstrate your skills and expertise.

9. **Soliciting feedback:** Seek feedback on your portfolio from colleagues, mentors, and industry professionals. Request constructive feedback and suggestions for improvement in order to improve the quality and effectiveness of your portfolio. Incorporate feedback and make adjustments as needed to ensure that your portfolio accurately reflects your ghostwriting skills and capabilities.

Marketing Yourself as a Ghostwriter

Marketing yourself as a ghostwriter is critical for attracting clients, developing your brand, and expanding your business in the competitive world of writing. Effective marketing strategies enable you to demonstrate your skills, expertise, and unique value proposition to potential clients, establishing yourself as a trustworthy and dependable ghostwriter.

Here's a thorough overview of how to market yourself as a ghostwriter:

1. **Define Your Brand:** Begin by establishing your personal brand as a ghostwriter. Identify your unique strengths, writing style, niche expertise, and the value you provide to clients. Create a compelling brand identity that speaks to your target audience and differentiates you from other ghostwriters in the industry.

2. **Build a Professional Website:** Establishing a professional online presence is critical when marketing yourself as a ghostwriter. Create a professional website or online portfolio that includes writing samples, client testimonials, services provided, and contact information. To attract potential clients, make sure your website is visually appealing, user-friendly, and search engine optimized.

3. **Create a Strong Online Presence:** Use digital marketing channels to broaden your reach and connect with prospective customers. Use social media platforms like LinkedIn, Twitter, Facebook, and Instagram to share your writing expertise, interact with your audience, and promote your work. Join online writing communities, forums, and groups to connect with other writers and potential clients.

4. **Create compelling content:** Create compelling content that highlights your writing skills and expertise. Write blog posts, articles, whitepapers, or guest posts about relevant topics in your niche to establish yourself as a thought leader in your field. Share your content on your website, social media platforms, and other online channels to attract and engage potential customers.

5. **Network and Develop Relationships:** Networking is essential for growing your clientele and developing relationships in the writing industry. Attend writing

conferences, workshops, and networking events to meet other writers, editors, publishers, and prospective clients. Engage in meaningful conversations, exchange business cards, and follow up with contacts to foster relationships and investigate potential collaboration opportunities.

6. **Use testimonials and case studies:** Use client testimonials and case studies to highlight your previous successes and satisfied customers. To gain the trust and credibility of potential clients, feature testimonials prominently on your website and in your marketing materials. Share success stories and case studies that demonstrate your expertise, problem-solving abilities, and positive results for clients.

7. **Provide free resources and samples:** Free resources, such as e-books, guides, or sample chapters, can help potential clients see your writing style and expertise. Offer free consultations or initial discovery calls to discuss potential projects and how you can assist with their writing needs. Providing valuable free content fosters trust and credibility among potential clients, encouraging them to hire you for their projects.

8. **Participate in Writing Workshops and Conferences:** Attend writing workshops, seminars, and conferences to improve your skills, broaden your knowledge, and connect with industry professionals. Take advantage of opportunities

to learn from experienced writers, editors, and publishers while also staying up-to-date on industry trends and best practices. Networking at writing events can also result in client referrals and collaboration opportunities.

9. **Invest in professional development**: Invest in continuous professional development to remain competitive in the writing industry. Take writing classes, workshops, or certifications to improve your skills and knowledge in specific areas of writing. Stay up-to-date on industry trends, tools, and technologies in order to provide the best services to your clients and stand out from the competition.

10. **Provide Exceptional Customer Service:** Provide exceptional customer service to your clients in order to establish long-term relationships and encourage repeat business. Communicate proactively, respond quickly to inquiries, and produce high-quality work that exceeds client expectations. Strive to give your clients a positive and seamless experience throughout the writing process, from initial consultation to project completion.

Managing Client Relationships

Managing client relationships is an essential part of being a successful ghostwriter since it has a direct influence on your ability to recruit clients, create high-quality work, and establish a great reputation in the industry.

Let's go over each component of maintaining client relationships in depth:

1. Building relationships: Establishing a solid relationship with clients entails making a personal connection and learning about their preferences and aspirations.

2. Maintaining Open Communication: Transparency is critical throughout the writing process. Keeping clients informed about project progress, updates, and issues helps to manage expectations and build trust. Responding to customer queries and delivering timely updates indicates professionalism and commitment to the project.

3. Understanding Client Needs: Understanding the client's vision, objectives, and target audience is critical to achieving good outcomes. You may guarantee that your work meets the client's expectations by having detailed talks and asking clarifying questions.

4. Managing Expectations: Setting reasonable expectations from the beginning helps to avoid misunderstandings and frustration later on. Clearly defining project scope, dates, and deliverables ensures that both parties are on the same page. Being open about your availability and constraints helps you manage client expectations efficiently.

5. Delivering exceptional service: going above and beyond to provide high-quality work that is consistent with the client's vision indicates your dedication to excellence. Providing innovative thoughts, being open to criticism, and allowing adjustments all help to ensure customer happiness and project success.

6. Managing Feedback and Revisions: Managing client feedback and revisions effectively is critical to maintaining a strong connection. Being receptive to feedback, implementing adjustments on time, and communicating effectively about any issues or restrictions demonstrates your professionalism and desire to satisfy client demands.

7. Resolving difficulties and concerns: Addressing any difficulties or concerns that occur during the writing process in a timely and professional manner is critical for maintaining customer satisfaction. Listening intently to client criticism, displaying empathy, and working cooperatively to discover solutions all contribute to dispute resolution and a strong working relationship.

8. Building Long-Term Relationships: Focusing on developing long-term relationships with clients entails encouraging regular contact and interaction. You may nurture a loyal customer base and encourage repeat business by getting in touch on a regular basis, exploring potential cooperation options, and expressing gratitude for client loyalty.

Techniques for Capturing Your Client's Voice

As a ghostwriter, capturing your client's voice involves sensitivity, observation, and the ability to adjust your writing style to your client's tone, vocabulary, and personality. By successfully capturing your client's voice, you can develop content that feels real and resonates with the audience, effectively delivering the client's message and accomplishing their objectives.

As a ghostwriter, you may capture your client's voice using the following techniques:

1. **Listen actively:** Effective communication is the key to capturing your client's voice. Listen actively during first talks, consultations, or interviews to learn about your client's personality, preferences, and communication style. Pay attention to their tone, vocabulary choices, and general manner to identify their distinct voice.
2. **Review Existing Content:** Analyze all content produced by your client, such as articles, blog entries, social media posts, and marketing materials. Examine the vocabulary, tone, and style utilized in their work to discover patterns and traits that constitute their voice. This will provide you with vital

insights into how they connect with their audience and help you mimic their tone in your writing.

3. **Conduct interviews or Surveys:** If feasible, do interviews or surveys with your customer to learn more about their voice and communication preferences. Ask open-ended inquiries that allow people to express their ideas, opinions, and personal experiences. Pay close attention to their word choice, storytelling style, and emotions in order to effectively reflect their voice.

4. **Provide quotations and examples:** To accurately portray your client's voice, use exact quotations or examples offered by them in your work. Include words, sentiments, or anecdotes that highlight their own personality and viewpoint. Integrating their own words into the narrative ensures consistency and authenticity in capturing their voice.

5. **Evaluate Audience Perceptions:** When creating content, it is important to consider how the audience will perceive your client's voice. Research their target audience's demographics, hobbies, and preferences before tailoring your writing style. Adapt the tone, phrasing, and level of formality to connect with the audience and meet their expectations while still expressing your client's voice.

6. **Collaborate, Iterate:** Work closely with your customer throughout the writing process to capture their voice

effectively. Share drafts or outlines for comments, and use their suggestions to improve the material. Be willing to make modifications and iterations to ensure that the final result correctly represents their voice and satisfies their expectations.

7. **Empathize with your client**: Put yourself in your client's position and understand their perspective, aspirations, and obstacles. Consider their objectives, beliefs, and unique selling qualities while creating content to express their real voice. Understanding their perspective and emotional context allows you to develop content that resonates with their audience and accurately portrays their voice.

8. **Pay attention to details:** Pay close attention to little aspects like word choice, phrase structure, and tone to authentically portray your client's voice. Mirror their linguistic preferences, employ terms specific to their sector or specialty, and tailor your writing style to their brand personality. Consistency in these aspects will help to create a cohesive and true representation of their voice. To summarize, as a ghostwriter, you must actively listen, be empathetic, observe, and pay close attention to detail.

Conducting Effective Interviews

Ghostwriters must be able to conduct good interviews in order to obtain useful information, thoughts, and viewpoints from their clients for use in their writing.

Whether doing interviews in person, over the phone, or via video conferencing, ghostwriters must properly prepare, ask appropriate questions, attentively listen, and change their technique to capture the client's voice and fulfill their writing goals.

Preparation: Before conducting an interview, ghostwriters must properly prepare. This includes investigating the client's background, industry, target audience, and project objectives. Familiarize yourself with any previous material created by the client, such as articles, blog posts, or speeches, to better grasp their voice, tone, and meaning. Create a list of questions or themes to lead the interview and ensure that you cover all pertinent areas.

Building rapport: Establishing rapport with the customer is essential for having a good interview. Begin by introducing yourself and stating the aim of the interview. Take the effort to establish a personal relationship with the customer by expressing genuine interest in their history, experiences, and viewpoints. Create a friendly and non-intimidating interview setting.

Asking open-ended questions: During the interview, use open-ended questions to allow the client to express their opinions, insights, and experiences in depth. Avoid asking yes-or-no or leading questions, as they may restrict the client's replies. Instead, ask probing questions that generate detailed responses, and encourage the client to provide examples, stories, and precise details to expand the discourse.

Active Listening: Active listening is an essential ability for ghostwriters during interviews. Pay great attention to the client's comments, nonverbal indicators, and emotional tone to acquire a better grasp of their viewpoint and communication style. Avoid interrupting the customer and instead allow them to fully express themselves before asking follow-up questions or requesting clarification.

Adapting Your Approach: Be flexible and adaptive when conducting interviews. Customize your inquiries and discussion style to match the client's preferences and communication style. Adjust the interview's pace, tone of voice, and level of formality to meet the client's comfort level and develop rapport. Prepare to pivot the discussion based on the client's comments and follow their lead to thoroughly explore pertinent issues.

Asking for Specific Information: Ask for particular facts, examples, and stories that can help you comprehend the client's point of view and inform your writing. Use follow-up questions to dive further into certain issues or clarify unclear points. Encourage the client to offer concrete examples, case studies, or personal experiences to support their claims and bring their ideas to life.

Summarize and clarify: Summarize and explain essential issues from the interview to ensure mutual comprehension and alignment. Recap key findings, themes, and action items to ensure you're on the same page as the customer. Seek clarification on any areas of ambiguity or doubt to avoid misconceptions and ensure that you correctly represent the client's vision.

Follow-up and Documentation: After the interview, thank the customer for their time and insights. Review your interview notes or recordings to ensure that you have accurately captured critical facts and significant takeaways. Organize and document the material obtained during the interview for future reference, and then use it to guide your writing process effectively.

Analyzing Existing Work for Voice and Tone

Analyzing current work for voice and tone is an important component of ghostwriting since it helps ghostwriters understand and replicate their clients' style, personality, and messaging. Ghostwriters can find patterns, themes, and features that characterize the client's style and tone by thoroughly reviewing their prior works, speeches, or other content.

Here's a complete and comprehensive summary of how a ghostwriter may examine previous work for voice and tone:

1. **Reviewing past Content:** Analyze any past content created by the client, such as articles, blog entries, social media postings, speeches, or marketing materials. Gather a diverse range of examples to gain a thorough knowledge of the client's writing style and communication preferences. Pay attention to the wording, tone, vocabulary, sentence structure, and general style of the client's writing.

2. **Identifying Patterns and Characteristics:** Examine the client's prior work to find patterns, themes, and traits that characterize their voice and tone. Look for any repeating phrases, statements, or rhetorical strategies utilized by the client. Take note of any distinguishing characteristics, such as humor, wit, sincerity, or authority, which add to the client's unique voice. Identify the

essential message points, values, and themes that appear regularly in the client's work.

3. Evaluate Audience Perception: Consider how the client's target audience sees their voice and tone in past content. Analyze audience feedback, comments, or responses to the client's work to see how well it connects with the intended audience. Pay attention to the audience's tone of participation, emotional responses, and overall perception of the information. This information enables ghostwriters to adjust their writing to effectively connect with the client's target audience.

4. Emulating Style and Language: Once you've recognized the major aspects of the client's voice and tone, try to emulate their style and language in your ghostwriting. Mirror the client's terminology, sentence structure, and rhetorical strategies to ensure that they keep their established voice. Use comparable language, tone, and phrasing to deliver messages that are consistent with the client's current brand identity and messaging.

5. Understanding Context and Purpose: When studying the client's speech and tone, keep in mind the context and purpose of their prior material. Understand the particular goals, objectives, and intended audience for each piece of content. Adapt your analysis to ensure that you capture the proper tone and voice for the context and goal of the writing.

6. Introducing Personalization: Incorporate customized pieces from the client's past work to increase authenticity and relevancy in your ghostwriting. Refer to particular tales, instances, or personal experiences offered by the customer in their prior material. By using these personal touches, you can develop content that seems genuine and connects with the client's target audience on a deeper level.

7. Seeking feedback and iteration: Seek input from the customer on your writing to verify that you've caught their voice and tone correctly. Share drafts or outlines of your work for assessment, and include any criticism or recommendations from the customer. Be open to iteration and refinement to ensure that the final result meets the client's expectations and appropriately represents their voice and tone.

8. Continuously Refine Your Approach: Continually improve your approach to analyzing previous work for voice and tone based on comments and project experience. Pay close attention to nuances, subtleties, and changing preferences in the client's voice and tone over time. Adapt your writing style and technique to remain relevant and successful in capturing the client's voice in your ghostwriting.

Using Tools and Resources to Understand Client Preferences

Ghostwriters must use tools and resources to discover their clients' preferences in order to provide material that is consistent with their vision, style, and objectives. Ghostwriters may acquire insights, analyze data, and adjust their writing to their clients' individual tastes by using a variety of tools and resources.

Here's a complete and comprehensive review of how ghostwriters may use tools and resources to efficiently grasp client preferences:

1. Client Surveys and Questionnaires: Create surveys or questionnaires to ask the customer directly about their project preferences, goals, and expectations. Include questions about their preferred writing style, tone, messaging, target audience, and expected results. Analyze the answers to learn about the client's preferences and modify your writing accordingly.

2. Client Interviews and Consultations: Conduct interviews or discussions with the customer to thoroughly understand their preferences, vision, and project objectives. Use open-ended inquiries to encourage the customer to express their views, ideas, and comments. Actively listen to their comments and offer probing questions to clear up any confusion or uncertainty. Use the collected information to inform your writing and ensure that it fits the client's expectations.

3. Analytical Tools and Data Analysis: Use analytical tools and data research approaches to learn about the client's target audience, market trends, and industry preferences. Conduct keyword research, competition analysis, and audience demographics studies to determine the language, subjects, and messaging that appeal to the target audience. Using this knowledge, you may customize your writing to successfully engage the client's audience and fulfill their goals.

4. Content Style Guides and Brand Guidelines: To better grasp the client's desired writing style, tone, and messaging, consult their content style guides, brand guidelines, or writing requirements. Learn about the client's brand voice, personality, and key message points to maintain consistency in your writing. Ensure that the customer's preferences are correctly met by following any specific rules or criteria they provide.

5. Client Feedback and Revisions: Seek feedback from the customer on your work to better understand their preferences and make any required modifications. Share drafts or outlines of your work for assessment, and include any criticism or recommendations from the customer. Be open to critical feedback and eager to iterate on your writing to ensure that it meets the client's preferences and objectives.

6. Collaboration and communication platforms: Use cooperation and communication systems to enable continuous discussion and idea exchange with the client. Use project management software, email, messaging applications, or video conferencing platforms to efficiently connect with the customer, give updates, and clarify preferences or needs. Maintain continuous communication to ensure that you are in sync with the client's preferences throughout the writing process.

7. Industry Research and Best Practices: Conduct industry research and study the best writing techniques to better comprehend current trends, norms, and preferences in the client's sector or specialty. Keep up with developing themes, popular content forms, and successful storytelling strategies relevant to the client's target audience. Use industry data and best practices to personalize your writing to the client's preferences and help them reach their goals efficiently.

Crafting Authentic Dialogue and Narratives

Creating authentic dialogue and narratives is a critical component of ghostwriting that necessitates a thorough grasp of character development, storytelling strategies, and the client's tone and vision.

As a ghostwriter, your job is to produce compelling and credible dialogue and storylines that connect with the audience while authentically reflecting the client's voice and messaging.

Here's a complete and comprehensive breakdown of how a ghostwriter may create authentic conversations and narratives:

To write effective conversations and narratives, it's important to first comprehend the characters in the story. This involves a comprehension of their personalities, goals, backgrounds, and interactions with other characters. Take the time to flesh out each character's unique traits, quirks, and speech patterns to ensure that their dialogue feels authentic and true to their character.

Emulating the Client's Voice: When crafting dialogue and narratives, it's crucial to emulate the client's voice and writing style to maintain consistency with their established brand persona. Study the client's previous work, including their writing samples, speeches, or public appearances, to understand their voice, tone, and messaging. Incorporate elements of their voice, such as vocabulary, sentence structure, and tone, into the dialogue and narratives to ensure that they align with the client's preferences and objectives.

Creating Believable Dialogue: Crafting believable dialogue involves creating conversations that sound natural and authentic while also serving the story's purpose and advancing the plot. Pay attention to the rhythm, pacing, and flow of the dialogue to ensure that it feels realistic and engaging. Use dialogue tags, gestures, and facial expressions to convey emotions, subtext, and character dynamics effectively. Avoid clichés, overly formal language, or unrealistic exchanges that can detract from the authenticity of the dialogue.

Developing Engaging Narratives: Crafting engaging narratives is essential for captivating the audience and immersing them in the story. Develop a compelling storyline with well-defined plot points, conflicts, and resolutions that keep the audience invested in the narrative. Use descriptive language, sensory details, and vivid imagery to create immersive settings and bring the story to life. Incorporate elements of suspense, tension, and surprise to keep the audience engaged and eager to continue reading.

Balancing Exposition and Action: Finding the right balance between exposition and action is crucial for maintaining the momentum of the story while also providing necessary background information. Integrate exposition seamlessly into the narrative through dialogue, internal monologue, or descriptive passages that reveal essential details about the characters, setting, and plot. Avoid lengthy exposition dumps that disrupt the flow of the story and opt for subtle, organic ways to convey information to the audience.

Capturing Emotional Depth: Crafting authentic dialogue and narratives involves capturing the emotional depth of the characters and the story. Explore the characters' internal thoughts, feelings, and motivations through introspective moments, inner monologues, and emotional reactions to events. Show, don't tell, when portraying emotions, allowing the audience to infer the characters' feelings through their actions, expressions, and interactions with others. Create emotional resonance by addressing universal themes and experiences that resonate with the audience on a personal level.

Incorporating Subtext and Nuance: Crafting authentic dialogue and narratives involves incorporating subtext and nuance to add depth and complexity to the story. Explore underlying themes, subplots, and character dynamics that add layers of meaning to the dialogue and narrative. Use metaphor, symbolism, and foreshadowing to create sub textual layers that enrich the story and invite deeper interpretation by the audience. Allow for ambiguity and complexity in the characters' motivations and relationships, reflecting the complexities of real-life human interactions.

Feedback and Revisions: Ensuring Voice Consistency

Feedback and revisions are essential parts of the ghostwriting process, ensuring voice consistency and alignment with the client's vision and goals. As a ghostwriter, receiving client feedback and effectively implementing revisions are critical for improving the writing and maintaining a consistent voice throughout the project.

Here's a detailed and thorough overview of how feedback and revisions help to ensure voice consistency in ghostwriting:

Understanding client expectations: Before beginning the writing process, make sure you understand the client's expectations for voice, tone, and messaging. Gather information about the client's preferences, brand persona, and target audience through initial conversations, consultations, or project briefs. Understand the client's expected writing style, language, and tone.

Seeking Comprehensive Feedback: Once the initial draft or outline is complete, solicit comprehensive feedback from the client to understand their thoughts, impressions, and suggestions for improvement. Give the client the opportunity to express their preferences, dislikes, and specific changes they would like to see in the writing. Encourage the client to provide specific feedback on voice consistency, tone, character portrayal, and overall alignment with their vision.

Actively listening and Responding: Consider the client's feedback and incorporate their concerns and suggestions into the writing. Be open to constructive criticism and willing to make revisions based on the client's feedback. Show empathy and understanding for the client's point of view, acknowledging their vision and goals while also offering your expertise and insights as a professional ghostwriter.

Maintaining voice consistency: During the revision process, prioritize voice consistency with the client's established brand persona and messaging. Pay attention to language choice, tone, style, and character voice to ensure they are consistent with the client's preferences. Refer to the client's previous work, style guides, or brand guidelines to help guide your revisions and ensure that the writing is consistent with their voice and messaging.

Strategic Implementation of Revisions: Implement strategic revisions to address the client's feedback while maintaining the writing's integrity and voice consistency. Prioritize revisions that are critical to aligning the writing with the client's vision and objectives, concentrating on character development, plot progression, dialogue authenticity, and overall narrative coherence. Be selective in incorporating revisions that improve the quality and effectiveness of the writing while maintaining voice consistency.

Seeking Clarity and Guidance: If the client's feedback contains ambiguity or uncertainty, seek clarification and guidance to ensure that you are accurately addressing their concerns and preferences. Schedule follow-up discussions or consultations with the client to go over specific revisions or areas of the writing that need more clarification. Proactively communicate with the client to ensure alignment and comprehension throughout the revision process.

Iterating and Refining: revise based on client feedback and refine writing until it meets expectations and maintains voice consistency. Prepare to go through multiple rounds of revisions as needed, taking feedback and making changes to ensure that the writing accurately reflects the client's voice and vision. Maintain open communication with the client throughout the revision process, providing progress updates and requesting approval for final revisions.

Final Review and Approval: Once the revisions are complete, review the writing one final time to ensure voice consistency and meet the client's expectations. Seek client approval on the final version of the writing before moving on to the next stage of the project. Address any remaining concerns or revisions requested by the client to ensure that the final product meets their expectations and goals.

Ghostwriting for Various Formats

Ghostwriting for various formats entails adapting writing skills to different mediums and platforms while maintaining the client's voice and meeting their goals. As a ghostwriter, you must be able to write effectively in a variety of formats in order to meet the needs of your clients and reach a diverse audience.

Here's a detailed discussion of ghostwriting in different formats:

1. Books and e-books: Ghostwriting novels and e-books necessitates a thorough understanding of storytelling, narrative structure, and character development. Ghostwriters, whether writing fiction or nonfiction, must collaborate closely with their clients to outline the book's content, develop the plot or outline, and write engaging prose that captures the reader's attention. Ghostwriters must also follow the client's voice and vision while ensuring that the writing is consistent, well-researched, and meets the expectations of the target audience.

2. Articles and blog posts: Ghostwriting articles and blog posts entails creating content that is informative, engaging, and targeted to the client's intended audience. Ghostwriters must conduct thorough research on topics, create compelling headlines and introductions, and present information clearly and concisely. They must also seamlessly integrate the client's voice and messaging into the writing while adhering to the tone and style guidelines of the publication or website.

3. Speeches and Presentations: Ghostwriting speeches and presentations requires storytelling, persuasive writing, and public speaking abilities. Ghostwriters must understand the client's message, audience, and goals in order to create speeches that are compelling, memorable, and impactful. They must also tailor the writing style to the client's delivery preferences and ensure that the speech connects with the audience intellectually and emotionally.

4. Social media content: Ghostwriting social media content entails creating posts, captions, and other content for sites like Facebook, Twitter, Instagram, and LinkedIn. Ghostwriters must understand the client's brand voice and messaging, as well as the distinct features of each social media platform. They must create engaging, relevant content that aligns with the client's overall social media strategy while adhering to platform-specific guidelines and best practices.

5. Marketing Materials: Ghostwriting marketing materials like brochures, flyers, press releases, and ads necessitates a combination of persuasive writing and creative storytelling. Ghostwriters must understand the client's target audience, brand positioning, and marketing goals in order to create compelling copy that motivates action and produces results. They must also tailor their writing style to the specific medium and audience, whether it is print, digital, or multimedia.

6. Site Content: Ghostwriting website content entails writing copy for landing pages, product descriptions, about pages, and other areas of a client's website. Ghostwriters must understand the client's brand identity, value proposition, and target audience in order to create informative, engaging, and search engine-optimized content. They must also follow best practices for web writing, such as using clear headings, bullet points, and calls to action, to improve readability and the user experience.

7. Scripts and screenplays: Ghostwriting scripts and screenplays necessitates a thorough understanding of narrative techniques, character development, and visual storytelling. Ghostwriters, whether writing for film, television, or video content, must collaborate closely with the client to create compelling storylines, dialogue, and scenes that captivate audiences. They must also follow industry standards and formatting guidelines to ensure that the writing reflects the client's creative vision and goals.

Writing Books: Fiction and Non-Fiction

Writing books, both fiction and nonfiction, is a complex endeavor that involves a thorough grasp of narrative, research, and audience interaction. As a ghostwriter, you must adjust your technique to meet the particular needs of the project while keeping voice consistency and matching with the client's vision and objectives.

Fiction writing: Fiction writing entails producing captivating storylines, well-rounded characters, and vivid environments that attract readers. As a ghostwriter, your major goal is to bring the client's narrative concept to life while remaining true to their voice and stylistic preferences.

This approach frequently begins with brainstorming sessions or client-provided ideas that serve as the basis for the story's structure, themes, and character arcs. To achieve voice consistency in fiction writing, immerse yourself in the client's universe and characters, paying great attention to their personalities, motives, and conversation patterns.

Capture the spirit of the client's voice with realistic dialogue, evocative descriptions, and narrative choices that are consistent with their vision. Incorporate customer input throughout the writing process to help enhance the story and ensure that it meets their expectations.

Non-fiction writing: Entails presenting factual information, personal experiences, or arguments in a clear and interesting way. As a ghostwriter, your job is to turn the client's skills, information, or experiences into a cohesive story that teaches, informs, or inspires readers. Whether you're writing memoirs, self-help books, or educational guides, you want to deliver the client's content clearly while preserving voice consistency.

To achieve voice consistency in nonfiction writing, immerse oneself in the client's subject matter, performing extensive research and interviews to obtain important material and perspectives. Structure the book logically and systematically, giving significant concepts, examples, and case studies to support the client's fundamental thesis or message.

 Use the client's voice and tone throughout the writing, using their unique perspective, experiences, and expertise to increase authenticity and trust. Feedback and revisions are critical elements in ghostwriting to maintain voice consistency and meet client expectations.

Throughout the writing process, obtain feedback from the customer on draft chapters, outlines, or summaries to measure their response and make any required changes.

Actively listen to the client's input and incorporate their recommendations while keeping the writing's integrity and voice consistent. When adopting revisions, prioritize improvements that improve voice consistency and correspond with the client's vision and goals.

Address any problems or inconsistencies raised by the customer, whether they relate to character development, story advancement, dialogue authenticity, or overall narrative coherence. Be open to constructive criticism and prepared to revise the writing to ensure that it appropriately expresses the client's voice and accomplishes the intended results.

Creating Compelling Articles and Blog Posts

As a ghostwriter, you must create entertaining and useful writing that resonates with your target audience while being true to the client's voice and objectives.

To write engaging articles and blog entries for a personal blog, corporate website, or online magazine, ghostwriters must first grasp the client's brand identity, target audience, and content objectives.

Understanding the client's objectives: Before creating articles and blog posts, it's critical to grasp the client's goals, target audience, and content plan. Work closely with the customer to determine the content's aims, such as informing, entertaining, educating, or persuading the audience. Understand the client's brand identity, messaging, and tone to ensure that the material is consistent with the overall brand image and voice.

Researching Topics Thoroughly: Thorough research is required for writing appealing articles and blog posts that deliver useful information and insights to the audience. Conduct in-depth research on the chosen topic, collecting relevant facts, statistics, examples, and expert views to back up the material. Use trustworthy sources and references to verify that the information supplied is accurate and reliable.

Creating Engaging Headlines and Introductions: The title and introduction are critical components of articles and blog posts because they affect whether readers will interact with the content. Create intriguing headlines that capture the reader's attention while effectively communicating the article's topic and value offer. Write intriguing beginnings that pique the reader's interest and give a preview of what to expect from the content.

How to Effectively Structure Content: Organize the material in a clear and logical order to improve reading and understanding. Break up the content with subheadings, bullet points, and numbered lists to help readers skim and comprehend the material. To keep readers engaged throughout the article or blog post, ensure that ideas flow smoothly and that paragraph transitions are seamless.

Writing in a conversational tone: Writers often use a conversational tone in articles and blog entries to engage and connect with readers. Write in a kind and approachable tone, utilizing terminology that is simple to comprehend and relevant to the intended audience. Avoid using jargon or highly technical language, since this may alienate readers and reduce the readability of the information.

Incorporating visual elements: Visual features like photographs, infographics, and videos may help articles and blog posts stand out and be more successful. Include appropriate graphics to help the viewer understand the written information and give it extra context or visual appeal. Maintain professionalism and credibility by ensuring that the graphics are of good quality, topical, and appropriately acknowledged.

With Call-to-Action (CTA): Articles and blog articles frequently contain a call-to-action (CTA) at the conclusion to encourage reader participation or action. Depending on the client's goals, the CTA may direct readers to make a comment, share the information on social media, subscribe to a newsletter, or go to a specific website. Create appealing CTAs that are consistent with the content and encourage readers to perform the intended action.

Crafting Speeches and Presentations

As a ghostwriter, you must combine narrative, compelling writing, and an awareness of the audience's and client's goals to create speeches and presentations.

Ghostwriters are essential for crafting engaging speeches and presentations that successfully express the client's message and resonate with the audience, whether they are writing for business events, conferences, or public speaking engagements.

To create effective speeches and presentations, it's important to first grasp the client's objectives and the event's purpose. Work closely with the client to determine the essential messages, topics, and goals that they want to convey to the audience.

Understand your target audience's demographics, interests, and expectations so you can adjust your material properly. To create informed and compelling speeches and presentations, conduct thorough research on the topic and target audience. Conduct significant research on the issue to obtain relevant facts, data, statistics, and examples to back up the client's argument.

Understand the audience's background, expertise level, and interests to ensure that the material speaks to them and meets their wants and worries. Creating a captivating story is key to engaging the audience during a speech or presentation. Create a coherent plot or framework to guide the viewer through the content in a logical and captivating way. Use narrative tactics, stories, and examples to highlight important themes and make the text more relevant and remembered.

Writing persuasive content: speeches and presentations try to influence audience thoughts, opinions, and actions. Create convincing content that speaks to your audience's emotions, values, and goals. Use rhetorical strategies like repetition, analogy, and metaphor to increase the persuasiveness of your text. Create clear and succinct messaging that the audience can grasp and remember.

Adapting to the Client's Voice and Style: As a ghostwriter, it's important to match the client's personality and brand while writing speeches or presentations. Examine the client's prior speeches or presentations to determine their speaking style, tone, and linguistic preferences. Include parts of their voice and style in the article to ensure authenticity and consistency. Using visual aids like slides, graphics, and videos may improve the efficacy of speeches and presentations by providing visual support and emphasizing important themes.

Collaborate with the customer to develop visually appealing and relevant visual aids that enhance the content and engage the audience. Ensure that visual aids are clear, brief, and easy to grasp, while minimizing clutter and distractions. To prepare for a speech or presentation, practice delivery and rehearse numerous times after writing the content. Work with the client to fine-tune the delivery, timing, and tone so that the message is successful and connects with the audience. Practice transitioning between slides or sections and anticipating audience questions or reactions.

Seeking feedback and changes is crucial for improving the speech or presentation and meeting the client's objectives. Solicit feedback from the client or other stakeholders to determine their reaction to the content and delivery. Actively listen to their opinions and implement any recommendations or changes to enhance the speech or presentation. Be receptive to critical feedback and eager to alter your material until it fulfills the client's expectations and goals.

Scriptwriting for Film and Television

Scriptwriting for cinema and television as a ghostwriter is a difficult and creative process that entails building fascinating storylines, establishing dynamic characters, and producing engaging dialogue.

Ghostwriters play a critical role in partnering with clients to bring their vision to life while complying with industry norms and satisfying the expectations of producers, directors, and audiences.

Understanding Client Vision and Objectives: The first stage in scriptwriting as a ghostwriter is to grasp the client's vision, objectives, and goals for the project. This entails engaging closely with the customer to discuss their ideas, concepts, and intended outcomes for the film or television series.

Understanding the client's concept is vital for generating a script that matches their creative vision and connects with the target audience. During the researching and brainstorming phase, ghostwriters actively engage in rigorous research and brainstorming sessions to develop the storyline, plot, and characters based on the client's vision.

Research may entail examining similar films or television programs, evaluating viewer preferences, and garnering inspiration from numerous sources. Brainstorming sessions help ghostwriters to create ideas, examine numerous story options, and establish a solid framework for the screenplay.

Crafting the Storyline and Plot: With a firm knowledge of the client's vision and objectives, ghostwriters construct the storyline and plot of the screenplay. This entails defining the primary story points, character arcs, and crucial events that move the narrative ahead. Ghostwriters work closely with the client to ensure that the plot matches their vision and integrates their intended themes and messages.

Developing Dynamic Characters: Dynamic characters are vital for captivating viewers and propelling the tale forward. Ghostwriters engage with the client to construct well-rounded characters with different personalities, motives, and conflicts. Characters should be sympathetic, multi-dimensional, and capable of changing during the course of the tale. Ghostwriters try to ensure that each character has a role in developing the story and adding to the larger narrative.

Creating engaging conversation: Engaging conversation is vital for bringing characters to life and attracting listeners. Ghostwriters work closely with the client to develop realistic and memorable dialogue that represents the personalities and connections of the characters. Dialogue should be natural, meaningful, and move the story while preserving the tone and style of the screenplay. Ghostwriters aim to establish a balance between exposition, action, and character interaction to keep spectators involved.

Adhering to Industry Standards: Ghostwriters must adhere to industry standards and formatting norms while creating screenplays for cinema and television. This involves following standard screenplay forms, conventions, and professional terminology. Ghostwriters also guarantee that the script satisfies the unique criteria of the media, whether it's a feature film, television pilot, or episodic series.

Receiving input and adjustments: Throughout the scriptwriting process, ghostwriters engage closely with the client to gather input and make adjustments as needed. This may take numerous rounds of changes to fine-tune the plot, characters, dialogue, and general structure of the screenplay. Ghostwriters are responsive to constructive criticism and work tirelessly to incorporate the client's suggestions while keeping the integrity of the screenplay.

Ghostwriting in the Digital Age: Social Media, Emails, and More

Ghostwriting in the digital era spans a wide range of platforms and channels, including social media, emails, blogs, website content, and more. As communication continues to change in the digital arena, ghostwriters play a critical role in helping individuals and organizations successfully express their message, manage their online presence, and interact with their target audience.

Here's a lengthy debate about ghostwriting in the digital age:

1. **Social Media:** Social media sites such as Facebook, Twitter, Instagram, LinkedIn, and Tik-Tok have become vital tools for personal branding, marketing, and communication. Ghostwriters aid customers in producing compelling social media posts, captions, and updates that connect with their brand identity and resonate with their followers. This requires knowing the client's voice and tone, maintaining up-to-date with current trends, and integrating visual aspects to boost interaction. Ghostwriters also help manage social

media accounts, schedule updates, and connect with followers to maintain a constant and active presence online.

2. **Emails:** Email remains a key form of communication in both personal and professional contexts. Ghostwriters aid clients in producing efficient email messages, including newsletters, promotional emails, sales pitches, and client interaction. This requires producing captivating subject lines, succinct and useful body content, and unambiguous calls-to-action. Ghostwriters guarantee that emails are customized, relevant, and suited to the recipient's requirements and tastes. They also assist clients in managing email campaigns, measuring replies, and evaluating email success indicators to enhance future interactions.

3. **Blogs and Website Content:** Blogs and website content are vital for generating credibility, establishing authority, and drawing visitors to websites. Ghostwriters collaborate with clients to generate compelling blog posts, articles, and website content that display their expertise, solve audience requirements, and promote interaction. This requires completing exhaustive research on relevant topics, optimizing content for search engines (SEO), and sticking to company rules. Ghostwriters also aid with content strategy formulation, content calendar planning, and content

distribution across numerous channels to optimize reach and effect.

4. **Digital Publications:** Digital publications, including online magazines, newsletters, and e-books, give opportunities for people and organizations to share useful material with their audience. Ghostwriters assist customers in publishing high-quality articles, features, and e-books that educate, entertain, or inform readers. This entails researching interesting subjects, conducting interviews with subject-matter experts, and creating appealing content that corresponds with the publication's style and audience preferences. Ghostwriters also aid with content editing, proofreading, and optimizing material for digital distribution and consumption.

5. **Video Scripts and Multimedia Content:** As video content continues to develop across platforms like YouTube, Vimeo, and TikTok, ghostwriters are increasingly responsible for creating screenplays and material for multimedia formats. This involves designing interesting video scripts, vocal scripts, and multimedia material that successfully deliver the client's message and engage the audience. Ghostwriters interact with clients to discuss concepts, build storyboards, and produce screenplays that grab viewers and drive action.

6. **Brand Messaging and Online Reputation Management:** In the digital era, having a strong brand presence and

controlling online reputations are crucial for individuals and enterprises. Ghost writers aid businesses in generating a consistent brand message across numerous digital platforms, including social media, websites, and online profiles. This entails defining brand voice standards, building appealing brand narratives, and ensuring that all communications connect with the company's values and objectives. Ghostwriters also monitor internet mentions, respond to consumer requests and criticism, and handle crises to safeguard and promote the client's online image.

Overcoming Challenges and Building a Successful Career

Overcoming hurdles and developing a successful career as a ghostwriter is a journey filled with ups and downs, but with determination, creativity, and strategic thinking, it's totally feasible to carve out a satisfying route in this dynamic sector.

Navigating the Competitive Landscape: One of the biggest hurdles for budding ghostwriters is navigating the competitive marketplace. The rise of digital platforms and self-publishing has saturated the market with writers vying for clients and projects. However, you can overcome this challenge by honing your unique voice, identifying your niche or specialty, and showcasing your expertise through a standout portfolio.

Establishing Credibility and Reputation: Establishing trust and reputation is vital for creating a successful career as a ghostwriter. Clients are more likely to trust writers with a proven track record of delivering high-quality work. To address this obstacle, focus on producing great outcomes on every project, accumulating testimonials and endorsements from delighted clients, and networking within the industry to create contacts with new clients and collaborators.

Balancing Creativity with Client Expectations: As a ghostwriter, you must combine your originality with the client's expectations and aims. This can sometimes be challenging, especially when clients have specific requirements or guidelines for their projects. However, overcoming this challenge involves effective communication with clients, asking clarifying questions, and offering creative solutions that align with their vision while staying true to your own voice and style.

Managing Time and Workload: Managing time and workload is another common challenge for ghostwriters, especially when juggling multiple projects or deadlines. To overcome this challenge, develop effective time management strategies, prioritize tasks based on deadlines and importance, and set realistic goals for each project. Additionally, consider outsourcing or delegating tasks when necessary to ensure that you can deliver high-quality work on time.

Dealing with Rejection and Criticism: Rejection and criticism are inevitable in any creative profession, including ghostwriting. It's essential to develop resilience and a growth mindset to overcome these challenges. Instead of dwelling on rejection or criticism, use them as opportunities for learning and growth. Seek feedback from clients and peers, identify areas for improvement, and continuously strive to enhance your skills and expertise.

Adapting to Industry Trends and Technology: New trends and technologies shape the way content is created and consumed in the constantly evolving writing industry. Ghostwriters must stay abreast of industry trends, such as the rise of digital publishing, audio content, and multimedia storytelling. Embrace new technologies and platforms that can enhance your writing skills and expand your reach as a ghostwriter.

Building a Sustainable Business Model: Building a sustainable business model as a ghostwriter involves overcoming various challenges, including setting competitive rates, negotiating contracts, and managing finances. To overcome these challenges, conduct thorough market research to determine industry standards for pricing and rates. Develop a clear pricing structure and contract terms that protect your interests while also meeting the needs of your clients.

Investing in Continuous Learning and Development: To overcome challenges and build a successful career as a ghostwriter, it's crucial to invest in continuous learning and development. Stay updated on industry trends, attend writing workshops and conferences, and seek mentorship from experienced writers. Continuously honing your skills and expanding your knowledge will not only help you overcome challenges but also position you as a top-tier ghostwriter in the industry.

Dealing with Writer's Block and Creative Challenges

Dealing with writer's block and creative obstacles is an unavoidable element of being a ghostwriter, since they can reduce productivity and stymie the creative process.

However, ghostwriters can use a variety of tactics and approaches to overcome these challenges and continue to produce high-quality work.

First and foremost, ghostwriters must recognize that writer's block is a typical occurrence among authors of all levels. Instead of viewing it as a sign of personal failure or weakness, ghostwriters must recognize that writer's block is a normal element of the creative process that can be efficiently controlled.

One effective way to overcome writer's block is to take a break and engage in activities that promote creativity and relaxation. This may include going for a stroll, meditating, practicing mindfulness, or taking up a non-writing interest. Taking a break from a project helps the mind recover and get new views, which may lead to increased creativity and productivity.

Another strategy is to divide the writing process into smaller, more manageable jobs. Rather than attempting to finish a complete article or chapter in one sitting, ghostwriters might establish smaller targets, such as writing a single paragraph or outlining crucial themes. This method reduces the pressure to produce perfect work while encouraging gradual development.

Including formal brainstorming sessions in the writing process might help produce new ideas and overcome creative obstacles. This might include generating thought maps, freewriting, or participating in collaborative brainstorming sessions with colleagues or clients. Ghostwriters might overcome creative blockages by exploring various viewpoints and perspectives.

Sticking to a steady writing pattern and carving out time for writing will help you overcome writer's block. Ghostwriters may educate their minds to identify particular times and locations with the act of writing by developing a consistent routine and a favorable writing atmosphere, making it easier to enter the flow state and overcome creative problems.

Seeking inspiration from other sources, such as books, movies, or music, may boost creativity and generate new ideas. Ghostwriters might get inspiration for their writing efforts by exposing themselves to a variety of situations and opinions.

When confronted with creative problems, ghostwriters should exercise self-compassion and avoid being overly harsh. Understanding that creativity ebbs and flows and that failures are a normal part of the process can help relieve stress and create a more optimistic and resilient attitude.

Balancing Multiple Projects and Deadlines

Ghostwriters frequently struggle to balance various assignments and deadlines, especially when working with many clients at the same time. Effective management of this area of the job necessitates careful planning, excellent organizational abilities, and the ability to prioritize duties efficiently.

Here's a lengthy overview of how ghostwriters may manage several assignments and deadlines:

1. Prioritize tasks: The first step in managing many projects and deadlines is to prioritize work based on urgency and priority. Determine which projects have upcoming deadlines and allocate time and resources accordingly. Decide the sequence in which to address the projects by considering their breadth and complexity.
2. Make a schedule: Creating a comprehensive timetable or timeline for each job might help ghostwriters keep organized and fulfill deadlines. Break down each job into smaller

pieces and set deadlines for completion. Use digital tools like project management software, calendar applications, and task management platforms to keep track of deadlines and progress.

3. Create realistic expectations: Ghostwriters must set reasonable expectations with customers for project schedules and deliverables. Be clear about your workload and availability to prevent overcommitting and ensure that deadlines are achievable. Communicate honestly with clients about any potential delays or issues that may develop throughout the project.

4. Use Time Wisely: Balancing various tasks and deadlines requires effective time management. Allocate specific time blocks for each project and prevent multitasking, since this can lead to poor productivity and quality. Set aside distractions and concentrate on one task at a time to increase efficiency and meet deadlines successfully.

5. Break down projects into manageable tasks: Breaking down huge projects into smaller, more achievable jobs might make them less daunting and simpler to complete. Create a project overview or checklist that includes all of the essential procedures and milestones for each project. This strategy enables ghostwriters to focus on one task at a time, resulting in a more ordered and systematic workflow.

6. Communicating Effectively with Clients: Maintaining open and honest communication with clients is critical when managing various projects and deadlines. Keep clients aware of work, updates, and any delays that might affect deadlines. Establish clear expectations for communication channels, response times, and deliverables to create a seamless working relationship.
7. Build Buffer Time: Building buffer time into project deadlines might help to avoid unforeseen delays or setbacks. Allow for extra time in project timelines to accommodate modifications, unanticipated client input, or unforeseen events that may develop throughout the project. This buffer period provides flexibility and ensures that deadlines can be met even in challenging circumstances.
8. Delegate Tasks Whenever Possible: If you have a lot of projects, consider assigning specific tasks to reliable colleagues or subcontractors. Outsourcing research, editing, or administrative work can free up time to focus on key writing obligations. Delegating duties enables ghostwriters to better manage their workload and achieve deadlines while maintaining quality.
9. Engage in self-care: Prioritizing self-care is critical while managing several projects and deadlines. Take frequent pauses, relax, and recharge to avoid burnout and stay

productive. Incorporate things like exercise, mindfulness, or hobbies into your daily routine to alleviate stress and maintain mental and physical health.

Handling Confidentiality and Discretion

Ghostwriters must maintain anonymity and discretion since they frequently deal with clients who do not want their name or involvement revealed. This component of ghostwriting necessitates a high level of professionalism, honesty, and ethical behavior in order to honor confidentiality agreements and sustain client confidence.

Ghostwriters must scrupulously follow the confidentiality and non-disclosure agreements (NDAs) negotiated with clients. These agreements establish the terms and circumstances for handling sensitive information, such as project details, client identification, and any proprietary or secret materials given by the client.

Ghostwriters must understand and follow these agreements completely, ensuring they do not disclose any secret material to third parties or use it for personal advantage.

Furthermore, ghostwriters must maintain secrecy while dealing with customers and other project stakeholders. This includes keeping a professional manner and abstaining from disclosing private project details or customer information to anybody other than the agreed-upon parties. Ghostwriters should be careful of their communication routes, making sure that project-related interactions take place in safe venues and platforms.

In addition to managing secret material, ghostwriters must manage scenarios in which they may come upon sensitive or contentious issues in their writing tasks. In such instances, ghostwriters must approach the subject with tact and respect for the client's preferences and limitations.

This might include obtaining clarification or assistance from the client on how to approach particular issues, as well as avoiding detailed information that could possibly violate confidentiality or hurt the client's reputation.

Ghostwriters must preserve their customers' intellectual property rights by guaranteeing that any written materials created throughout the project remain the client's property. This contains all drafts, outlines, research materials, and other items created throughout the cooperation. Ghostwriters should not keep copies of their work or use them for personal or professional reasons without the client's express authorization.

Building Long-Term Relationships with Clients

Building long-term connections with customers is critical for ghostwriters seeking a secure and sustainable profession. Building these relationships requires trust, communication, dependability, and the ability to consistently produce high-quality results.

Here's a complete and comprehensive way to develop long-term customer connections as a ghostwriter:

1. **Communication:** Effective communication is the foundation of any successful customer relationship. Ghostwriters must create open lines of communication with their customers from the start, ensuring that they understand the project's needs, timelines, and expectations. Regular and honest communication throughout the project promotes confidence and ensures that all parties are on the same page regarding the project's progress and possible obstacles.
2. **Understanding the Client's Needs:** To develop a long-term connection with a customer, ghostwriters must first grasp their requirements, interests, and ambitions. This includes asking probing questions, carefully listening to feedback, and tailoring their approach to the client's individual needs. Ghostwriters may establish themselves as trust-worthy

collaborators by showing a genuine interest in knowing and meeting the demands of their clients.

3. **Consistent quality of work:** Consistently producing high-quality work is critical for establishing trust and confidence with clients. Ghostwriters must attempt to maintain a high level of writing, fulfill deadlines, and provide content that meets or exceeds the client's expectations. Ghostwriters can build long-term connections with customers by constantly producing outstanding work.

4. **Reliability and Dependability:** Clients search for reliability and dependability when hiring a ghostwriter. Ghostwriters must demonstrate their devotion to the project by meeting deadlines, reacting quickly to client interactions, and proactively resolving any concerns that may emerge. Ghostwriters may acquire a reputation for trust and dependability by continuously delivering on their commitments and exceeding customer expectations, which is critical for developing long-term client relationships.

5. **Flexibility and adaptability:** Ghostwriters who engage with customers on a long-term basis must be flexible and adaptable. Client objectives and project requirements might vary over time, and ghostwriters must be able to adapt while preserving the quality of their work. This might include accepting modifications, incorporating customer comments,

or modifying project timeframes as required. Ghostwriters may create trust and confidence with customers by exhibiting flexibility and adaptation, resulting in long-term relationships founded on mutual respect and collaboration.

6. **Offer Value-Added Services:** Ghostwriters might offer services other than writing to differentiate themselves and bring value to customers. This might involve research support, content strategy formulation, editing and proofreading services, or advice on publication and distribution. Ghostwriters may position themselves as useful collaborators and establish long-term partnerships based on mutual success by providing complete solutions that suit the client's larger demands.

7. **Showing professionalism and integrity:** Professionalism and honesty are essential components of developing long-term relationships with clients. Ghostwriters must always behave professionally, respecting confidentiality, sticking to ethical norms, and following the terms of any agreements or contracts. Ghostwriters may gain trust and credibility by exhibiting professionalism and honesty in their dealings with clients, laying the groundwork for long-term partnerships based on mutual respect and trust.

Continuously Evolving as a Ghostwriter: Professional Development

As a ghostwriter, you must always evolve in order to remain relevant, improve your talents, and compete in the ever-changing writing profession.

Professional development is an important part of this journey, involving a variety of activities and tactics targeted at improving writing skills, extending knowledge, and adjusting to changing trends and technology. Continuous learning and education are essential components of ghostwriters' professional development.

This entails remaining current on industry trends, best practices, and emerging technology in a variety of ways, including attending seminars, webinars, and conferences, enrolling in writing courses or programs, and engaging in online forums and communities for writers. Ghostwriters may broaden their skill set, stay up-to-date on industry advancements, and remain competitive in the marketplace by actively exploring opportunities to learn and grow.

Another crucial part of professional growth is improving writing abilities and strategies. This involves writing on a regular basis, trying various genres and techniques, and seeking feedback from peers, mentors, or writing organizations. Ghostwriters can also branch out into specialty writing fields like content marketing, SEO writing, and copywriting to broaden their skill set and serve a wider range of customers and projects.

Networking and developing contacts within the writing community are also essential for professional growth. This entails interacting with other authors, editors, publishers, and industry experts via networking events, social media platforms, and online groups. Participating in discussions, sharing experiences, and seeking advice from peers may bring important insights, support, and chances for cooperation and progress.

Additionally, remaining current on industry tools and technology is critical for ghostwriters to remain competitive in the digital era. This involves becoming acquainted with writing software, productivity tools, and internet platforms widely utilized in the writing business. Keeping up with new tools and technology may help to simplify workflows, increase productivity, and improve the quality of work generated.

Furthermore, professional growth for ghostwriters entails constantly seeking criticism and self-evaluation. This involves asking clients, peers, and mentors for feedback on finished projects, actively exploring chances for development, and reflecting on prior experiences to discover areas for progress.

Ghostwriters can recognize strengths and limitations, make improvement objectives, and always seek to develop their abilities and knowledge by accepting feedback and self-assessment. Finally, professional growth for ghostwriters involves remaining flexible and open-minded in the face of change.

The writing industry is always changing, with new trends, technology, and customer preferences influencing the environment. Ghostwriters must be willing to adapt to these changes, seize new possibilities, and constantly improve their writing style to match the changing demands of customers and audiences.

Conclusion

Becoming a successful ghostwriter requires more than just mastering the craft of writing. It requires a thorough understanding of the industry, the ability to navigate various genres and styles, and a dedication to professionalism and ethical behavior.

Throughout this book, we've looked at the many aspects of ghostwriting, including understanding the role of a ghostwriter, honing writing skills, managing confidentiality, developing long-term client relationships, and constantly evolving through professional development. Ghostwriting is a dynamic and challenging field that provides numerous opportunities for writers with diverse backgrounds and skills.

Mastering the skills and strategies outlined in this book, aspiring ghostwriters can navigate the industry's complexities, build successful careers, and make significant contributions to the world of literature and publishing.

As you begin your journey to becoming a ghostwriter, remember to approach each project with professionalism, integrity, and a dedication to producing high-quality work. Stay curious, keep learning, and seize the challenges and opportunities that come your way. With dedication, perseverance, and a love of storytelling, you can carve out a rewarding and fulfilling career as a ghostwriter.

www.ingramcontent.com/pod-product-compliance
Lightning Source LLC
Chambersburg PA
CBHW071939210526
45479CB00002B/739